C000119593

Shambolic Mammal

Poems, lyrics, wordplay and musings
by
Jude Simpson

illustrated by: **Julie Shaw, Lydia Brown, Christine Lafon, Katy Brown**

malcolm down

PUBLISHING

First published 2022 by Malcolm Down Publishing Ltd.
www.malcolmdown.co.uk

24 23 22   7 6 5 4 3 2 1

British Library Cataloguing in Publication Data
A catalogue record for this book is available from the British Library.

ISBN 978-1-915046-22-2

Cover design by Angela Selfe
Art direction by Sarah Grace

Printed in the UK

Contents

Reptile Needs
illustrated by Julie Shaw, with an introduction, footnotes, and out-takes

5

Oh! No! My Baby is a Mango!
illustrated by Lydia Brown, with chords, melody and performance notes

25

Pink Lady
illustrated by Christine Lafon, with footnotes and out-takes

47

Parent
illustrated by Katy Brown, with a personal note

75

Reptile Needs

illustrated by

Julie Shaw

Reptile

This poem was inspired when I was driving with a friend past an out-of-town shopping complex. One of the huge, warehouse-like buildings had a sign on its side announcing that it was an Aquatics Centre. It proudly declared, "For All your Pet and Reptile Needs!"

A small shiver went down my spine, and I turned to my friend, who was driving. "I didn't know I had reptile needs," I confessed, breathily. It sounded rather exciting, full of untapped potential and permission to do exotic, unexpected things. So I decided to get in touch with my reptile needs . . . and this is the result . . .

I'm a shambolic mammal who feels like the dregs.
I've got too many arms, or not enough legs.
and something within me just wants to lay eggs[1].
I have reptile[2] needs!

---

1. The difference between laying eggs and ovulating is a great discussion to have.
2. There are two illustrations that are, in fact, non-reptilian – can you identify them?

I need to languish[3] in rivers and pools,
yeah, languishing's good, but I'm not a fool,
I also need a semi-nocturnal schedule
(if that's ok...?)

---

3. I love the feel of **'languish'** in my mouth – it requires effort but in a lazy, decadent sort of way, like physical onomatopoeia. That's why I repeated it almost immediately.

I need to get hotter, I need to get wetter,
I need to stop dithering – slithering's better.
I need to be scaly and toenaily too.
I need to be snakey and wakey and woo.

I need cold blood and I need hot sand.
I need a claw instead of a hand.
I need a claw and somewhere to stand
on four of them . . .

lithering

I need to learn lessons from turtles and lizards,
walk on the ceiling like some kind of wizard.
Would I get less wind if I ate with a gizzard?
Who knows?!

I need a long tongue and some hard, horny heels,
teeth that snap, a skin that peels,
and unhookable jaws for swallowing meals
that are larger than my head.
(Excellent![4])

---

4. I do genuinely enjoy large meals. In a restaurant once, I was publicly accused by a fellow female diner of having eaten a 'man's meal'. "*And you ate ALL OF IT!*" she inveighed, somewhat aggressively, but I suspect with a secret jealous admiration.

I need to chill out and be frequently sedentary,
swallow a hamster then just smile benevolently.
I need to do this[5] ... slightly more elegantly.
These are my reptile needs.

5. At this point, when performing the poem, I drop to the floor on all fours, and imitate a lizard lifting its diagonally-opposite pairs of legs alternately in what some people call a "lizard dance." It always gets a laugh from some people and a disbelieving "what-*ON-EARTH*-is-she-doing" look from others. It hasn't yet caused an injury . . .

Oh I don't need a lover, I don't need a pet,
I don't need a doctor, I don't need a vet,
I just need my reptile needs to be met (to be met)
(to be met) – *Is there a gecko in here?*[6]

6. This bit is fun to perform, faking the echo, then looking around the upper corners of the room in puzzlement before saying the gecko line. It usually gets both a laugh <u>and</u> a groan simultaneously! What a treat!

I need blood that warms when I lie in the sun,
rotating eyes and a curlier tongue.
I need them! I do! They're not just nice-to-haves!
I need to not mind where I go to the lav.

I need to not care if I live in a zoo.
I need to be more like them and less like you[7]!
I need to be fonder of my inner anaconda[8] –
the bond with my reptile self must be stronger.

I need a tail, or something to twitch.
I need to be scratched where my reptile needs itch,
and if you're asking ...

---

7. No offence.
8. or, 'Anna Conda,' the well-known snake-charmer.

I could do with a bit more basking.

Basking

Dead Darlings

Stephen King, in his book, "On Writing," talks about "killing your darlings" – editing out parts of your writing, even sacrificing some that you <u>really, really love</u>, in order to make the piece as a whole the best it can be[9].

Here are some of my dead reptilian darlings, still loved as they languish on the cutting-room floor . . .

---

9. Even this paragraph was originally twice as long . . . but I didn't have space in the book for the out-takes edited out of the out-takes . . .

When a dragonfly flew on the breeze past my eye, and
my mouth watered, tongue curled and flicked him inside,
I realised that I could no longer deny
my reptile needs.

Sedentary

A good set of spines would make me feel calmer,
and much more in touch with my reptile nirvana.
It was here a moment ago – now where's iguana?
My reptile need!

        I don't care for birdsong or music of whales.
           I just want to practice my reptile scales.

I don't need a counsellor or mentor befriending me.
I need eyes that rotate independently.

I crave colour-changing, chameleon skin,
'cause where I end up, I love to blend in,
and when you can't see me, my skin gets the credit,
though when it's too heavy, it'd be nice to shed it.

Yeah every so often, I'd quite like to say, 'hey,
this skin's got me bored now' and shrug it away,
but when I do that, the question is tough –
do I slough[10] my skin, or do I slough ?

---

10. the first is pronounced to rhyme with 'Slough', the town, the second with 'stuff'.

Languish

Right now, hibernation is sounding like a <u>really</u> good option.

Oh! No! My Baby Is A Mango!

illustrated by

Lydia Brown

I have four children.

That's my own fault, I'm not blaming you.

When I was pregnant with my eldest child, I had some very odd dreams, especially when the birth was getting closer. My most memorable dream was of going through all the machinations of childbirth, only to give birth to a mango.

The strange thing was, when the mango came out, I don't remember feeling disappointed, exactly. But it did make me realise that I'd subconsciously been piling up all sorts of dreams and ambitions for my child's life (possibly for my own benefit) and I remember feeling all of those expectations quickly melt away . . .

Spoiler alert: when I gave birth IRL it was actually a human, and a boy.

The doctor was Chris Witty,[11]
he was eating chicken korma.
A shadowy figure in a hat
stood in the corner
looking suspiciously
like the man from Del Monte.
He raised a can of Lilt at me
and whispered, "Santé" …

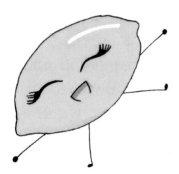

---

11. This piece was written some years ago. The first line was originally, "The Doctor was Nick Clegg in clogs, eating chicken korma." If you remember that, congratulations; you're officially a long-term fan and I officially love you.

They gave me a Mojito,
"so the pain is not too ghastly!"
Well, that was never mentioned
in my ante-natal classes!
But the birth was pretty easy –
I barely had to push
before a little bundle popped out
with a singsong, "whoosh![12]"

---

12. It's never been like that in real life – not for me, anyway . . .

I said, "is it a boy or girl?"
but the midwife frowned at this,
and said, "I think it's – no, it can't be –
argh! What do you think, Chris[13]?"
But Witty said, "it's not my thing,
soft fruit, I must confess."
So they asked the man
from Del Monte,
and he said ... "yes!"

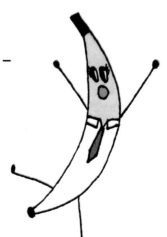

---

13. "frowned a bit // and said [...] Nick"

Oh! No! My baby is a mango!
He'll never be an architect.
He'll never dance the tango.
Ah! Me! It's not how things should be.
Oh! No! My baby is a mango!
He'll never be Prime Minister
or asked to join a quango.
Ah! Zut! A tropical fruit!
The doctors say they're mystified,
my baby is a mango ...

Well, experts came from far and wide
to peer and prod and pat me
and one particularly tactless one said,
"they're very good in chutney!"
But the obstetrician said, "it's great!
And while we're on the topic,
it seems Miss Simpson that your womb
is humid like the tropics ...!"

Oh! No! My baby is a mango!
He won't go all the places that
a real baby can go.
Ah! Me! It's not how things should be.
Oh! No! My baby is a mango!
He won't go off to travel,
or get casual work in Nando's.
Ah! Zut! A tropical fruit!
The doctors say they're mystified,
my baby is a mango . . .

It seems I'm not the only one –
my poor friend Mary-Sue
went through fifteen hours of labour
just to pop out a pack of Danish Blue!
But that's not the worst one –
no, there's more –
my friend Beverley gave birth
to her Father in Law ...!

Oh! No! My baby is a mango!
He'll never camp in France or learn
to dance a mean fandango.
Ah! Me! It's not how things should be.
Oh! No! My baby is a mango!
He'll never buy a sturdy tent from
Berghaus or from Vango.
Ah! Zut! A tropical fruit!
The doctors say they're mystified,
The doctors say they're mystified ...

Well, they <u>were</u> pretty mystified, those poor doctors –
I mean, imagine seeing someone give birth to a tropical
fruit, that is very un-**lychee** to happen! It took me a while
to **fig**-ure it out myself! I said to my Dad, I said "**papa-
ya** not gonna believe this . . . !" I felt sorry for myself at
first. "Poor me," I thought, **"pawpaw** me . . ." But then
I thought, "I'm gonna love my baby and I don't **guava**
damn what anyone else thinks!"

My baby is the fruit of passion,

but he is not a passionfruit...

He is a Mango!!!!

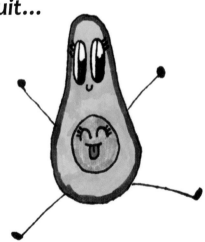

Oh! No! My baby is a mango!
He won't get into sourdough
or learn to play the banjo.
Ah! Me! It's not how things should be.
Oh! No! My baby is a mango!
He'll never eat a *Tarte Aux Pommes*
then say, 'where did that flan go?'
Ah! Zut! A tropical fruit!
The doctors say they're mystified,
my baby is a mango . . .

The Music

I perform this song with a first-fret capo. I've written the actual chords, with the fingering in brackets. Verses are spoken over the chords, the chorus is sung.

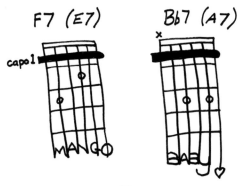

F7 (E7)   Bb7 (A7)

The Doctor was Chris Witty, he was eating chicken korma.

F7 (E7)   Bb7 (A7)

A shadowy figure in a hat stood in the corner

F7 (E7)   Bb7 (A7)

looking suspiciously like the man from Del Monte.

F7 (E7)   Bb7 (A7)

He raised a can of Lilt at me, and whispered, "Santé" ...

etc.

Performance notes:

This is a very surreal and bonkers song, so I like to have surreal and bonkers expressions on my face while I sing it.

The E7 / A7 combo helps create a sort of latino / tropical / curious / other-worldly atmosphere, so I start playing these chords as I introduce the song, talking about my surreal mango dream.

There is great scope for comical dismay with the "Oh No!", "Ah, Me!" and "Ah, Zut!" which are accented and half-spoken (I think the musical term is *recititavo*), and also for saying, "a tropical fruit" in a pouty, disheartened, big-eyed, French accent.

I enjoy playing this song with my friend Paul[14], who is much better at me than playing the guitar, and also has a fine range of surreal and bonkers facial expressions. We enjoy making the tropical fruit puns go on for ages, getting worse and worse, trying to keep a straight face, or trip up the other person with a new one you just thought of ...

I find great joy in the effort I put into crafting the performance of essentially nonsensical and superficially inconsequential pieces of song and poetry. The enrichment I appear to be able to bring to an audience by doing this proves, I believe, the nobility of silliness.

---

14. Paul Bell – an excellent, entertaining musician, who also made up some of the puns.

And just in case you really haven't had enough of those tropical fruit puns . . .

Water-melon-choly look you had on your face, Jude, when that happened.

Yes, Paul, but then I decided I was going to love my baby, **kumquat** may . . .

Well done you, Jude – I can see from your face that you're now feeling quite sub**lime**.

That's true, Paul, in fact, I feel like singing!! ♪ *I've got the **kiwi**, I've got the secret . . .* ♪

Will you put him in a bassinet, Jude, or maybe an **apri-cot**?

Paul, these puns are so bad, they're making me **quince**!

I know Jude, we're really **plum**-ming the depths now.

A plum isn't even tropical, Paul!

DAMson!

Pink Lady

or

Goodbye thrifty housewife, hello consistently satisfying apple-eating experience!

illustrated by

Christine Lafon

I want to dine on an apple tonight.
Many vie for my attention, but there's only one that's right.
Others barely get a mention after this love at first sight –
I pick you!

You're smooth and shiny, you're circular and neat –
Your flavour's a life-saver, naturally sweet.
A crunch without corners, no tricks with this treat –
I pick you.

Golden delicious isn't crisp enough, I say.
Pippins and Coxes, in your flippin' boxes stay!

Can I call you Rosy? Promise you won't stray –
I pick you.

You're hardly ever maggoty, you gladden me, you see.
You can prove theories of gravity by falling from a tree.
You send me to the lavatory if I eat more than three –
I pick you!

You're spherical, not ovally. You're really just an ovary.
Are you good in a breakfast that's granola-ry? Yeh, totally!
Glossy and sleek (ooh) that's the way you flow to me –
devotedly unwrinkled and not at all scrotum-y[15].

---

15. Sorry.

Don't shilly shally, dilly dally with my meal!
You're never peely-wally til you're peeled – such appeal!
you're my purée of sunshine, my cider-ffect, ideal –
I pick you!

Unashamedly blush, I must be flush to afford you –
curves like a corm, for your form I applaud you.
If you were a juice I would be the one who poured you.
If you were a magician's beautiful assistant I would be
the one who sawed you
in half and then in quarters, then cored you,
and absorbed you
into my digestive system.[16]

---

16. What is a metaphor for, if not pushing too far . . . ?

Secure in your pink finery,
you're not male or non-binary,
but will you take a shine to me –
'cause if you do, that's fine by me –
a sign that you're aligned with me,
inclined to be refined like me,
or . . .

      . . . just have too much time, like me,
      to contemplate the comparative virtues
      of different varieties of orchard fruit. Shoot!

Oh, but talking of shooting,
don't Tell William,
but I'd aim to offer up
several billion
for your shade of pink.
It's clearly not vermilion,
or scarlet like the poisoned one
that tempted Snow White,
or golden like the Trojan one
that started that fight.

You're much more civilian,
conciliating,
your pink's not a silly one
to start wars willy-nilly, it's a
coral,
prawnish,
krilly one ...

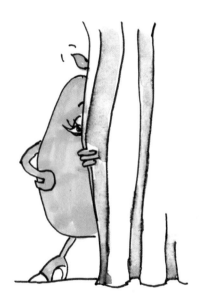

Apples and Gentlemen,
lend me your ears!
You're the lady of my eye!
Motherhood and pink pie!
You pip me to the post!
I love you to the core!
I would pluck you from the jaws
of a roasted wild boar.

"Shall we get out of here?"
– just planting a seed.
If something crops up,
chop chop, show some speed.
Don't stem this tide of love –
pack a trunk, take a bough.
Let's turnover a new life,
branch out, say ciao!

Let's upset the cart,
be desserters in the raw,
'cause without you I'd crumble
and without me you're slaw.

We could cut a figure, make it big in New York,
'cause I didn't quite twig
til you said, "take my stalk, and let's walk,
bite the bullet – the time's ripe to roll."
Let's leaf in the morning . . .

...I'll pick you up from the fruit bowl.

These segments were cut and discarded ...

I spurn a Braeburn, a Jazz is just a has-been.
You stoke up my dopamine, so can I start a fanzine –
kicking up a can-can in the canteen –
I pick you![17]

---

17. It gives me a proper tingle when I get alliteration, internal rhyme and double-syllable end-rhyme/assonance all working. Look – spurn/burn, Brae/burn, jazz/just, jazz/has, stoke/dope, been/zine/teen, kick/pick, kick/can, can/can/can ... But you can't include something simply on the basis of its technical satisfactoriness. No player is bigger than the team ...

Not tart enough for Tatin, no, you're much more satiny.
I'd gladly take you out to a Saturday matinée.
You're rounded and firm but not nearly as fat-as-me –
you flatter me.

You're curvier than Tinkerbell.
I think you wouldn't sink as well –
if dropped into a sink, you would bob around
                                    and wink as well.

You're generously sized, not a tiddly pomme.
I'll be your chomping cheerleader, cheering you on
with my pompoms.

You're not a Ten Pound Pom[18], – more like £2.80 for a pack
of six.

You're the 'sauce' of my happiness![19]

---

18. I quite liked this, because the Pink Lady was originally cultivated in Australia.
19. Interesting how some homophones work best written, others prefer being spoken . . .

This apple isn't Adam's, no you're much more ladyish –
smooth-skinned and round like a bottom that is babyish –
grown up in a place that is sheltered and shadyish.
You're not a baby fish . . .

Don't turn to jelly!

I don't need a manly one
when you're my hypanthium[20]

---

20. I learnt this word writing this poem. From the Greek, "under the little flower."

A worm would never reach ya,
you're too good for a teacher,
Oh no, what I meant is,
you keep away the dentist.

Pink, green and groovy,
you're wasted in a smoothie,
you move me, you soothe me,
I'm your snoozy foodie . . .

Parent

illustrated by

Katy Brown

I've been …

A nappy changer
A bottlefeeder
A nap giver
A nap needer
A breastfeeder
A story reader
I've been a breeder.

I've been

A snuggler
and a swaddler
A cuddler
Not a mollycoddler
A caresser
and a cradler
A success
and a failure.

"Waa Waa"

I've been

A desperate-for-routine-er
                    and an on-demand feeder
A big bed sharer
                    and a "go sleep over there-"er
A let-them-cry-it-out
                    and a come-at-the-first-peep.

I've been . . .

A night-time pacer
An up-every-hour-er
A picker-up, a putter-down, a picker-up-er, putter-down-er
picker-up, a putter-down, a hair-tearer-out-er
Befuddled, addled, muddled, maddened
No need to count sheep

Sometimes I've not even known

Whether I'm awake or asleep.

I've been . . .

A tidier-up and a mess maker too
A potty-trainer, an explainer of the loo
A clearer up of explosive poo

A snot wiper
A snot ignorer

A snot-not-even-noticing-your-snot-any-more-er . . .

A catcher of the falling

A comforter of the bawling

A path-clearer for the crawling

A referee of the brawling.

I've been . . .

A lego builder
A tracker, a trainer
A *'yes, I'd love to dress up as a fairy with you'* claimer
A waiter
and a caterer
An expert
and an L-plater

A tooth wobbler
A tooth extricator
A tooth fairy
And a tooth fairy myth propagator.

I've made Nativity costumes
and a mask for spiderman
I can make the international space station out of
two shoe boxes and an empty pringles can.

I've been your leader, team-mate, witness
and your "Mummy, go away!"
I've been desperate for you to start school
and I've been choking back a tear on your first day...

I've been...

A form filler-in-er
A slip tearer-off-er
A PE kit rememberer
A white shirt washer

$2 + 9 = ?$

A reading record ticker
A sticker sticker
An expert in the exploits
of Biff, Chip and Kipper.

A suncream applier
A school shoe buyer
A *'when did your feet get that big?!'*
crier.

A playground natterer
A time sacrificer
A get-involved
and a not-on-your-lifer

A hapless spender
A purse-strings tightener
An art critic – *'that's beautiful, darling ... what is it?'*
and an art recycler ...

I can bake a cake for the PTA
with half an hour to go
I can show amazement
at the same badly-performed magic trick
fourteen times in a row

I've said 'yes' and I've said 'no'
I've said 'that's brilliant'
I've said 'well done'
I've said 'I love it'
I've said 'not now'
And I've said 'ok, only once'

"No"

"Brilliant"

"I love it!"

"Not now!"

I've said '*louder*' and I've said '*shush*'
I've been strict and I've been a pushover
I've said '*not in those shoes*'
              'never in the house'
                    '*only in the bath,*' and
'<u>not</u> *while it's attached to the hosepipe!*'

I've been…

A gift giver and a confiscator
Your prison guard and your liberator
Your social worker, perker-upper
Romance adviser
and commiserator

Your cleaner, cook and laundrymaid
Your headache and your health
The person who does everything for you
Then makes you do it yourself.

I've been your tutor and your teacher
By the book and off the page
Your preacher, friend, beseecher, housekeeper
All unpaid.

Your party planner, taxi driver
Storer, co-explorer
Shoulder-crier, shoelace-tier
Watcher and ignorer

A whisperer, a listener
A ruler and a flouter
A peacekeeper, a battler
A *'will-you-get-your-stuff-together-*
so-we-can-leave-the-house' shouter
A doubter of myself
A comparing comparee
Driving myself mad with how-does-she-do-its
while others say the same about me.

I've been

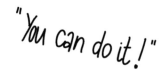

A fearer for your happiness
A confident cheerleader
An optimist, a despairer
a *'don't be embarrassed of your own mum'* pleader

An encourager and a nagger
A defender and a bragger
A praiser and a corrector
A pusher-forward and a protector

I've said *'stand on your own feet'*
And *'come here for a hug'*
I've put my foot down, held you in my arms
and let you blub.

I've looked into your baby eyes
Now you tower above me
I've sat outside the door you slammed
And prayed for you to love me.

I've been ...

Infuriated, nauseated, in tears, beyond tears, exhausted, laughing and crying, insane and in love at the same time.

I've been ignored, dismissed, disrespected, and taken for granted.

It's ruined me, aged me, wrinkled me and greyed me, it's wrung me out and hung me up and left me high and dry

but you know what the really crazy thing is? –
If you ask me what I'd change, I will always say,

not a single thing.

Because

just occasionally

I've been ...

Waved to
Run to
Searched for
Sung to
Wished for
Kissed
Missed
and clung to.

I've been . . .

       Leapt upon

       Clutched

       Cuddled up to and

       Hugged

       Hand-gripped

       Face-nuzzled

       Hair-stroked

       Bugged.

I've been …

Longed for
Waited for
Rushed towards
Stampeded
Loved
unconditionally
Needed.

I've been…

Listened to
Confided in
Trusted
Believed
Told *'I'm sorry'*
Told *'I love you'*
Heard your secrets
Known your dreams.

I've seen you open your eyes
when it's time to be found
I've been the finger for your
tiny little hand to curl around
The cord that gave you nourishment
The belly where you were forming
I've been jumped on
with a home-made birthday card
at quarter to six in the morning.

I've been ...

     The centre of your universe

     The corner for your fight

     Your first port of call and

     Your last face at night

     Your nearly perfect hero

     Your sunshine and your shade

     It's been the best job in the world

     A million times overpaid.

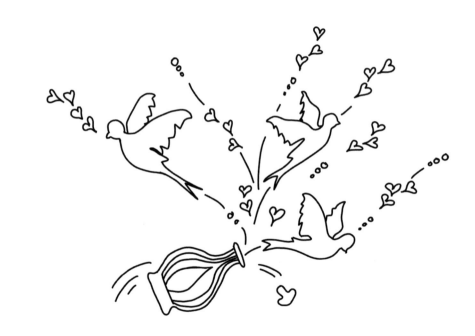

I've been . . .

> Chosen, called
> and honoured
> I've been
> Privileged
> and blessed
> Appointed, prized
> Anointed, flawed
> Adored and called the best.

I've known you

loved you

and released you

and now that's all I've got to show

that I've been

a parent.

What more does anyone need to know?

This poem had many starting points.

One was my work with Homestart, as Poet in Residence of my local branch. I've been privileged to work with Homestart for some years now, and have seen their extraordinary service to families in crisis, via their well-trained and whole-hearted volunteers. Thank you. I'm honoured to work with you and support you.

Another starting point was the number of times I hear parents (usually Mums) who are mainly or wholly home-based carers being asked, "what do you do?" and struggling to reply. It's not easy to sum up how you spend all your time caring for others, providing for your children, looking after your family, taking care of your home, often responding to needs in the community. It pains me deeply when women are ever embarrassed, under-certain or apologetic about a decision to base themselves at home, mainly working to nurture their families. I wish that every woman (or man, or parent) genuinely had that choice, knew they had that choice, and had the freedom and agency to exercise that choice.

There often comes a time when a parent decides to spend more hours in paid work, or to return to a career after having had a period of mostly looking after children. When that happens, I often hear them wondering what they can put on their CV, what skills they have – after all, they've "just" been a "full-time Mum," haven't they?

This poem is perhaps an attempt to write that CV. It's an articulation and celebration of the many varied and even contradictory tasks we carry out as parents. It's an acknowledgement of the painful but wonderful truth that our ultimate success criterion is our children leaving us.

I rarely describe myself as a feminist. Which is a shame. But this is my strongest feminist view: that people <u>must</u> value the skills and time spent in work that is traditionally viewed as female, and continues to be vastly overlooked in its importance in building and holding together a society. This work is generally unpaid or low-paid, unseen, or unsung. We can't measure it in the traditional 'male,' ways – money, KPIs, out-put or numbers. Yet it is work, and without it, our world has very little chance of ever reflecting the best of humanity.

In this I include people looking after other people's children for a few pounds an hour, and striving to do an excellent job while those around them complain about the cost of childcare. I include all different types of parents; care workers; nursing staff who provide excellent nurturing care; parents at home with disabled children, parents caring for disabled adult offspring, parents in a full-time job so that they can afford the best, or possibly only decent school provision for their special-needs child; foster parents; adoptive parents; anyone who take somebody's children off their hands so they can go for dinner, or enjoy a bike ride, or just breathe. People who did not or could not become parents, so pour out their nurturing instincts in other directions. I include anyone who visits a lonely person, talks to them, takes them out. Anyone who helps run a youth group. Anyone who listens to somebody whose speech or thought processes or difference mean that patience, time and energy are required to really hear them. In short, anyone who uses their own personal and emotional resources to value someone else's quality of life, with little or no recognisable reward. Maybe one day I'll write a poem about how angry this all makes me. But for now, enough of the politics. Bless you. May your work be fulfilling, and may you never look back and regret time you didn't spend with other people. And I hope you enjoyed this poem, and all the poems.

Jude x

Julie Shaw is a musician, director of music, music teacher, composer, calligraphist, crafter and artist based in Surrey. She designs Celtic knotwork and fulfils commissions for cards, wedding stationery and commemorative artwork.

Katy Brown is a Mother of three and Pre-school teacher, who also produces doodle art, undertaking personalised commissions, especially for weddings and baby arrivals.

Facebook: Life in Doodles

Christine Lafon is a self-taught artist based in Cambridge. She exhibits regularly with Cambridge Drawing Society and Open Studios. Her work, though figurative, is spiced with distinctive abstract touches.

www.christinelafonart.co.uk/
Facebook: Christine Lafon Art.

Lydia Brown is ten years old. She loves art, fashion, make-up, writing, dancing and sweets.

Youtube

Instagram

Contact Page/
Mailing List